We designed The Hopework book to be used alongside the Hopeful Minds Deep Dive Curriculum, free for download at www.hopefulminds.org. We encourage you to use this program at home, in school, place of worship, during after-school programs, with police teaching youth programs, or anywhere where there are groups of people eager to activate hope.

No special training is required to use our Hopework book, as it was tailored for all age groups. While the book was written for anyone who can read English, parents, caregivers, or teachers may need to assist young children who are still learning to read.

Our workbook can be used with any population. We believe hope is a skill anyone and everyone should develop, as research has found hope to be impactful in many areas of life. We ALL need to know how to proactively manage hopelessness and have skills to activate hope.

While you work through the materials, we ask that you share the images from the workbook on social media, to help us learn and inspire others on the 'how' to hope. Tag **@ifredorg** and use hashtags **#HopefulMinds #Hope #SHINEHope #FiveKeysToSHINEHope #GrowHope** as you post. For our younger users, make sure to get parent permission prior to posting anything on social media. Thank you for choosing hope not only for yourself, but for those who share and teach along the way. Together, we can improve our collective future hope is key to creating all we want.

*These materials are designed to assist you in learning about hope and implementing hope-based curriculums in a classroom setting. They should not be used for medical advice, counseling, or other health-related services. iFred and Hopeful Minds do not endorse or provide any medical advice, diagnosis, or treatment. The information provided herein should not be used for the diagnosis or treatment of any medical condition and cannot be substituted for the advice of physicians, licensed professionals, or therapists who are familiar with your specific situation. Consult a licensed medical professional, or call 911, if you are in need of immediate assistance.*

© 2020, Innovative Analysis, LLC. Distributed by the International Foundation for Research and Education for Depression (iFred), www.ifred.org.

# HOPE SCALES

What you cannot measure, you cannot improve. It is therefore important to measure your hope levels to monitor your progress and check in on yourself. While there are many scales for hope, we use the Children and Adult Snyder Hope Scales to measure hope, as they have been used in many studies on hope. By taking the Snyder Hope Scale regularly, you can begin to see the link between hope and outcomes in every area of your life.

Hope is a journey; as you move forward, your hope levels will rise and fall. That is okay. If you practice your hope skills regularly, no matter how hopeless life seems in the low moments, you will always have a way back to hope.

We ask that you measure your hope, and encourage all those in your community to measure hope, so we can start tracking hopefulness in individuals around the world. As you work through the Hopeful Minds curriculum, consider administering the hope scale multiple times so the students can keep track of their hope level changes.

Use the link provided to take the Snyder Hope Scale Assessment *(if you are under 18, make sure to get adult permission before accessing the internet)*:

www.hopefulminds.org/hope-scales

**My current Snyder Hope Scale Score:** ☐ / 64

**How do you feel about your score?**
_____
_____

**How hopeful have you been in your life?**
_____
_____

**How has your hope impacted your ability to achieve goals?**
_____
_____

**In what areas of your life do you feel like you could be more hopeful?**
_____
_____

This course teaches you the hope skills you can use to create, maintain, and grow hope. There will be times throughout your life when you or someone you love experiences hopelessness. It is at these times, when your hope score is at its lowest, that it is most important to practice skills to activate hope.

The goal of this course is to learn the "how-to" of hope so that you can both create a model for your own life and share the power of hope with others.

**Who in your life could benefit from higher hope?**
_____
_____

**What organizations or businesses in your community could benefit from learning about hope?**
_____
_____

# STRENGTHS FINDER

Understanding your strengths is another important tool for creating and maintaining hope. Focusing on your strengths can help you manage your stress response, cultivate positive thoughts, and focus on the future. Additionally, understanding strengths allows one to capitalize on their strengths while moving toward inspired actions, a necessary element in hope. Use this tool with yourself, and others. We want to focus on the children's strengths as opposed to what they are doing wrong because recognizing strengths in children can help them build confidence and support their life-long pursuit of hope. As you continue through this workbook, you will repeatedly be asked to reflect on your strengths. It is a positive way to create a more hopeful future.

You can check out your strengths here *(if you are under 18, make sure to get adult permission before accessing the internet)*:

**hopefulmindsets.pro.viasurvey.org**

**Write down the top five strengths from your results:**

1 _____   4 _____

2 _____   5 _____

3 _____

**Which of these strengths do you think is most tied to your ability to grow and maintain hope?**
_____
_____

**Are you activating your strengths regularly? How so?**
_____
_____

**How can you better utilize your strengths in different areas of your life?**
_____
_____

## LESSON 1 WORKSHEET
# DEFINE HOPE

Please tag us on social media @ifredorg to share your completed work and use the hashtags: #HopefulMinds #Hope #SHINEHope #FiveKeysToSHINEHope #GrowHope #WhatAndWhyofHope

# MY HOPE SUNFLOWER

**Directions:** Fill in each section of your Hope Sunflower.

#HopefulMinds #Hope #SHINEHope #FiveKeysToSHINEHope
#GrowHope #WhatAndWhyofHope #HopeSunflower

LESSON 2 WORKSHEETS

# WHY IS HOPE IMPORTANT

Please tag us on social media @ifredorg to share your completed work and use the hashtags: #HopefulMinds #Hope #SHINEHope #FiveKeysToSHINEHope #GrowHope #WhyIsHopeImportant

# A MESSAGE ABOUT HOPE

**Directions:** Tape or write your message in the space below.

# HOPE WORKSHEET

**Directions:** Fill in each box with a drawing or 1-3 sentences of writing.

**Draw something you are hopeful for:**

**I hope for:**

**Hope is important because:**

#HopefulMinds #Hope #SHINEHope #FiveKeysToSHINEHope #GrowHope #WhyIsHopeImportant #ImHopefulFor

LESSON 3 WORKSHEET

# THE BRAIN AND HOPE

Please tag us on social media @ifredorg to share your completed work and use the hashtags: #HopefulMinds #Hope #SHINEHope #FiveKeysToSHINEHope #GrowHope #BrainAndHope

# MY BRAIN

**I. Directions:** Fill in the blanks with the emotions of the emoticon facial expressions that match using *fear, anger, sadness, relaxed, happy, and excited.*

**II. Directions:** Draw how your body feels when you are in your upstairs and downstairs brain.

#HopefulMinds #Hope #SHINEHope #FiveKeysToSHINEHope #GrowHope #BrainAndHope #MyHopeBrain

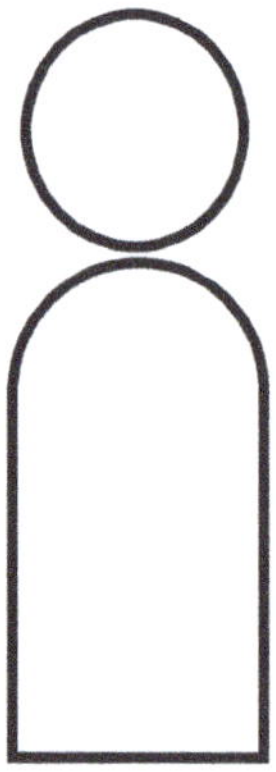

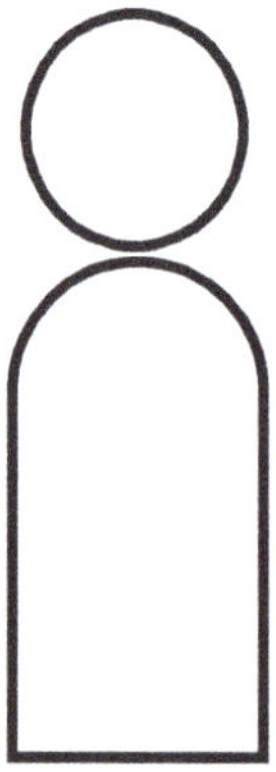

# Feelings Chart

This was reproduced with the permission of Friendship Bench. See all of their amazing work, and learn how to bring a friendship bench to your community at www.friendshipbenchzimbabwe.org

LESSON 4 WORKSHEET

# IDENTIFYING HOPEFUL EMOTIONS

Please tag us on social media @ifredorg to share your completed work and use the hashtags: #HopefulMinds #Hope #SHINEHope #FiveKeysToSHINEHope #GrowHope #IdentifyingHopefulEmotions

# 90 SECOND STRATEGIES

**Directions:** Fill in each row based on the emotion in the left column.

| Emotion | Last Time I Felt This Way | Where I Feel it in my Body | Where I feel it in my brain | 90 Second Strategies to Calm Down |
|---|---|---|---|---|
| SAD | | | ▲ UPSTAIRS ▼ DOWNSTAIRS | |
| ANGRY | | | ▲ UPSTAIRS ▼ DOWNSTAIRS | |
| AFRAID | | | ▲ UPSTAIRS ▼ DOWNSTAIRS | |
| SCARED | | | ▲ UPSTAIRS ▼ DOWNSTAIRS | |
| HOPELESS | | | ▲ UPSTAIRS ▼ DOWNSTAIRS | |

*#HopefulMinds #Hope #SHINEHope #FiveKeysToSHINEHope #GrowHope #IdentifyingHopefulEmotions #90SecondStrategies*

## LESSON 5 WORKSHEET
# CREATING A HOPEFUL MINDSET

Please tag us on social media @ifredorg to share your completed work and use the hashtags: #HopefulMinds #Hope #SHINEHope #FiveKeysToSHINEHope #GrowHope #CreatingAHopefulMindset

# HAPPINESS HABITS

**Directions:** Fill in each blank with 1-3 words.

### 3 THINGS I'M GOOD AT:
1. _____
2. _____
3. _____

### 3 THINGS I LIKE ABOUT MYSELF:
1. _____
2. _____
3. _____

### 3 THINGS I LIKE DOING:
1. _____
2. _____
3. _____

### 3 THINGS THAT MAKE ME LAUGH:
1. _____
2. _____
3. _____

### 3 THINGS I'M GRATEFUL FOR:
1. _____
2. _____
3. _____

### 3 THINGS I'M EXCITED FOR:
1. _____
2. _____
3. _____

*#HopefulMinds #Hope #SHINEHope #FiveKeysToSHINEHope #GrowHope #CreatingAHopefulMindset #HappinessHabits*

LESSON 6 WORKSHEET

# PRACTICING HAPPINESS HABITS

Please tag us on social media @ifredorg to share your completed work and use the hashtags: #HopefulMinds #Hope #SHINEHope #FiveKeysToSHINEHope #GrowHope #PracticingHappinessHabits

# PRACTICING GRATITUDE

**Directions:** Fill in each blank with 1-3 words

Three things you are grateful for about yourself:

1. _____
2. _____
3. _____

Three things you are grateful for about someone in your life:

1. _____
2. _____
3. _____

Three things you are grateful for that happened today:

1. _____
2. _____
3. _____

*#HopefulMinds #Hope #SHINEHope #FiveKeysToSHINEHope #GrowHope*
*#PracticingHappinessHabits #Practicing Gratitude*

## LESSON 7 WORKSHEETS
# WONDER AND AWE

Please tag us on social media @ifredorg to share your completed work and use the hashtags: #HopefulMinds #Hope #SHINEHope #FiveKeysToSHINEHope #GrowHope #HopeWonderAndAwe

# SEVEN WONDERS OF THE WORLD

### GREAT WALL OF CHINA

**Location:** China
**Fun Fact:** The Great Wall is 13,107 miles long and can be seen from space.

### THE COLOSSEUM

**Location:** Rome, Italy
**Fun Fact:** The Colosseum is in the middle of Rome and was originally built for gladiator contests.

### PETRA

**Location:** Jordan
**Fun Fact:** This city of stone buildings carved into the cliffs has been inhabited since 7000 B.C. - over 9,000 years.

### CHICHEN ITZA

**Location:** Mexico
**Fun Fact:** The city of Chichen Itza was built by the Mayans almost 1500 years ago. The pyramids in the city are lined up with stars and planets in the sky.

### MACHU PICCHU

**Location:** Peru
**Fun Fact:** Machu Picchu is located at the very top of an 8,000-foot high mountain. When it was built in the 1400s, it took people four days to climb to the city.

### TAJ MAHAL

**Location:** India
**Fun Fact:** The Taj Mahal was built by an emperor in 1632 to hold the tomb of his favorite wife.

### CHRIST THE REDEEMER

**Location:** Brazil
**Fun Fact:** This giant statue is at the top of a hill overlooking the city of Rio de Janeiro. It took 100 people and 60,000 pieces of stone to build it.

# EIGHTH WONDER OF THE WORLD

**Directions:** Use your imagination to design a new Wonder of the World. Draw the monument in the space below, and then answer the questions.

**IF YOU COULD DESIGN AN 8TH WONDER OF THE WORLD, WHAT WOULD IT LOOK LIKE:**

WHERE IS YOUR EIGHTH WONDER LOCATED?
_____
_____

WHAT IS A FUN FACT ABOUT YOUR EIGHTH WONDER?
_____
_____

WHY DOES YOUR EIGHTH WONDER MAKE PEOPLE FEEL WONDER AND AWE?
_____
_____

HOW DOES YOUR EIGHTH WONDER INSPIRE HOPE?
_____
_____

*#HopefulMinds #Hope #SHINEHope #FiveKeysToSHINEHope #GrowHope #HopeWonderAndAwe #HopeWonderOfTheWorld*

# PERSPECTIVE JOURNALING

**Directions:** Listen to the prompt from your teacher, and then write down what you observe from different perspectives.

**The world as I see it:**

_____
_____
_____
_____
_____
_____

**The world as an ant would see it:**

_____
_____
_____
_____
_____
_____
_____
_____

**The world as the bird would see it:**

_____
_____
_____
_____
_____
_____
_____
_____

#HopefulMinds #Hope #SHINEHope #FiveKeysToSHINEHope #GrowHope #HopeWonderAndAwe #HopePerspectiveJournaling

## LESSON 8 WORKSHEETS

# PASSION, PURPOSE, AND HOPE

Please tag us on social media @ifredorg to share your completed work and use the hashtags: #HopefulMinds #Hope #SHINEHope #FiveKeysToSHINEHope #GrowHope #PassionPurposeHope

# THINGS I AM PASSIONATE ABOUT

**Directions:** Draw or make a collage of things that you are passionate about in the space below.

#HopefulMinds #Hope #SHINEHope #FiveKeysToSHINEHope #GrowHope #PassionPurposeHope #ImPassionateAbout

# PURPOSE MIND MAP

**Directions:** Use the Mind Map Template or free area below to create a Mind Map of your passions and purposes.

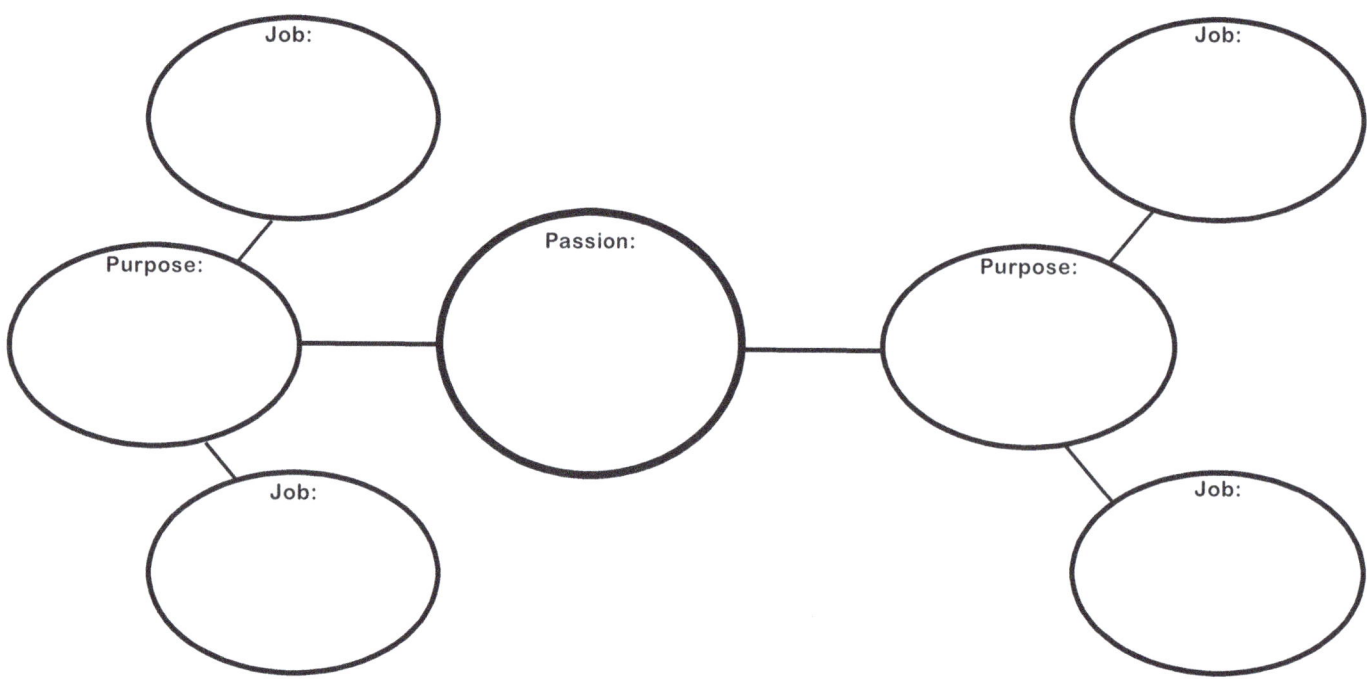

**How will I know I have achieved success?**
_____
_____

#HopefulMinds #Hope #SHINEHope #FiveKeysToSHINEHope #GrowHope #PassionPurposeHope #PurposeMindMap

**LESSON 9 WORKSHEETS**

# REVIEWING HOPE

Please tag us on social media @ifredorg to share your completed work and use the hashtags: #HopefulMinds #Hope #SHINEHope #FiveKeysToSHINEHope #GrowHope #ReviewingHope

# MY HOPE SUNFLOWER (SECTION 2)

**Directions:** Fill in each section of your Hope Sunflower.

# HOPE OVERVIEW

**I. Directions:** Answer each question in the space provided.

## ALL ABOUT HOPE:

**WHAT IS THE DEFINITION OF HOPE?**
_____

**WHAT ARE THE TWO INGREDIENTS OF HOPE?**
_____

**WHY IS HOPE IMPORTANT?**
_____

**II. Directions:** Write where in your brain (upstairs brain or downstairs brain) you feel each of these emotions.

## THE BRAIN AND HOPE:

**HAPPINESS** _____

**SADNESS** _____

**FEAR** _____

**ANGER** _____

**HOPE** _____

**III. Directions:** List three Stress Skills and Happiness Habits that you use in your life.

## THE BRAIN AND HOPE:

| STRESS SKILLS | HAPPINESS HABITS |
|---|---|
| 1. _____ | 1. _____ |
| 2. _____ | 2. _____ |
| 3. _____ | 3. _____ |

#HopefulMinds #Hope #SHINEHope #FiveKeysToSHINEHope #GrowHope #HopeOverview

# CREATING HOPE FOR A NEW SEMESTER

**Directions:** Fill in the boxes below with 1-5 words each. Check all the boxes that apply to your goal, then explain how your goal meets each SMART criteria.

WHAT IS ONE THING I AM HOPEFUL FOR?

ONE STRESS SKILL I WILL USE THIS SEMESTER IS:

ONE HAPPINESS HABIT I WILL USE THIS SEMESTER IS:

ONE THING I AM PASSIONATE ABOUT:

ONE PURPOSE I HAVE:

## LESSON 10 WORKSHEET

# PURPOSEFUL GOALS FOR HOPE

Please tag us on social media @ifredorg to share your completed work and use the hashtags: #HopefulMinds #Hope #SHINEHope #FiveKeysToSHINEHope #GrowHope #HopeGoals

# THE WOOP METHOD

## WOOP stands for:

### Wish
Think about your purpose. What is an important wish that you have for your purpose? You want to pick a wish that is challenging, but that you can still fulfill.

### Outcome
What would be the best possible outcome if your wish came true? How would fulfilling your wish make you feel?

### Obstacle
What is one obstacle that might make it hard to reach your wish?

### Plan
Identify one action you can take or thought you can think to overcome your obstacle. Then, make an if-then plan: IF (I encounter this obstacle) THEN (I will use this solution).

# SMART GOALS FOR SUCCESS

 **S**PECIFIC — Be specific about your goal. Think about these questions when creating your goal: What needs to be accomplished? Who is responsible for it? What steps will you take to achieve it?

 **M**EASURABLE — Can you measure your progress? If this goal will take a long time to achieve, set shorter term goals to reach along the way.

 **A**CHIEVABLE — Are you inspired and motivated to reach your goal? Do you have the tools or skills you need? If not, do you know how you can get them?

 **R**ELEVANT — Does your goal make sense? Does it go along with what you are trying to achieve in the bigger picture?

 **T**IME-BOUND — Is your timing realistic? Can you achieve your goal in the time period set? Think about what you may want to achieve at the halfway point.

# THE WOOP METHOD AND SMART GOALS

**Directions:** Fill in the boxes below. Use your purpose to practice the WOOP Method.

**PURPOSE**

Write down a WOOP for your purpose:

**W**ISH

**O**UTCOME

**O**BSTACLE

**P**LAN

#HopefulMinds #Hope #SHINEHope #FiveKeysToSHINEHope #GrowHope #HopeGoals #WOOPHope #SMARTHope

# THE WOOP METHOD AND SMART GOALS (CON'T)

**Directions:** Now that you have your WOOP, use it to create a SMART Goal. Check all the boxes that apply to your goal, then explain how your goal meets each SMART criteria.

## GOAL:

IS IT:  HOW?

- **S**PECIFIC  _____
- **M**EASURABLE  _____
- **A**CHIEVABLE  _____
- **R**ELEVANT  _____
- **T**IME-BOUND  _____

## STEPS I'LL TAKE TO REACH THAT GOAL:

1. _____
2. _____
3. _____
4. _____
5. _____

*#HopefulMinds #Hope #SHINEHope #FiveKeysToSHINEHope #GrowHope #HopeGoals #WOOPHope #SMARTHope*

LESSON 11 WORKSHEETS

# A HOPEFUL APPROACH TO CHANGE

Please tag us on social media @ifredorg to share your completed work and use the hashtags: #HopefulMinds #Hope #SHINEHope #FiveKeysToSHINEHope #GrowHope #HopefulApproachToChange

# OBSTACLES AND SOLUTIONS

**Directions:** Fill in each blank with 1-5 words describing an obstacle you might encounter and a solution to that obstacle.

**SMART GOAL:** _____

**OBSTACLE # 1**
_____
_____

**SOLUTION**
_____
_____

**OBSTACLE # 2**
_____
_____

**SOLUTION**
_____
_____

**OBSTACLE # 3**
_____
_____

**SOLUTION**
_____
_____

**MY SMART GOAL**
_____
_____

*#HopefulMinds #Hope #SHINEHope #FiveKeysToSHINEHope #GrowHope*
*#HopefulApproachToChange #HopeObstaclesAndSolutions*

# REEVALUATING SMART GOALS

**Directions:** Write down a SMART goal and, using the emotions it makes you feel, identify a new SMART goal.

**SMART GOAL:**

**OBSTACLE I CAN'T OVERCOME:**

Circle the feelings that are associated with this goal:

| | | |
|---|---|---|
| Happiness | Excitement | Pride |
| Contentment | Successfulness | Joy |
| Connection | Serenity | Love |
| Accomplishment | Enthusiasm | Calm |

**BRAINSTORM:** What are other things that make me feel these emotions?

1. _____
2. _____
3. _____

**NEW SMART GOAL TO REACH THESE EMOTIONS:**

*#HopefulMinds #Hope #SHINEHope #FiveKeysToSHINEHope #GrowHope*
*#HopefulApproachToChange #SMARTHope*

LESSON 12 WORKSHEETS

# CREATING A NETWORK FOR HOPE

Please tag us on social media @ifredorg to share your completed work and use the hashtags: #HopefulMinds #Hope #SHINEHope #FiveKeysToSHINEHope #GrowHope #HopeNetwork

# NOURISHING NETWORK

**Directions:** Write or draw answers to each of the prompts below.

Friends and family I can count on and confide in:
_____
_____

People I turn to for Stress Skills:
_____
_____

People I practice Happiness Habits with:
_____
_____

Things I can connect to:
*ex. Spiritual Advisor, Peer Support, Animals, Nature, etc.*
_____
_____

Teachers, doctors, and experts I go to for support:
_____
_____

Community Resources I can utilize:
_____
_____

Where can I go to in times of crisis?
*ex. If you can't list anyone, you can check out our list of resources for how to get connected.*
*Visit https://hopefulcities.org/get-support/*
_____
_____

One person I can always count on even if we aren't close: [                                    ]

#HopefulMinds #Hope #SHINEHope #FiveKeysToSHINEHope #GrowHope #HopeNetwork #NourishingNetwork

# MY HOPE STORY

**Directions:** Use the space below to write a "Hope Hero Spotlight" about yourself.

*#HopefulMinds #Hope #SHINEHope #FiveKeysToSHINEHope #GrowHope #HopeNetwork #MyHopeStory*

LESSON 13 WORKSHEET

# STRENGTHENING HOPE NETWORK WITH EMPATHY

Please tag us on social media @ifredorg to share your completed work and use the hashtags: #HopefulMinds #Hope #SHINEHope #FiveKeysToSHINEHope #GrowHope #StrengthenHopeNetwork

# PUTTING MYSELF IN THEIR SHOES

**Directions:** Fill in each blank below with 1-5 words or emotions.

## THE LAST TIME SOMEONE WAS UNKIND TO ME:

### HOW I FELT:

### HOW THEY MIGHT HAVE FELT:

### HOW THEY COULD HAVE SHOWN EMPATHY:

### HOW I COULD HAVE SHOWN EMPATHY:

## THE LAST TIME I WAS UNKIND TO SOMEONE ELSE:

### HOW I FELT:

### HOW THEY MIGHT HAVE FELT:

### HOW THEY COULD HAVE SHOWN EMPATHY:

### HOW I COULD HAVE SHOWN EMPATHY:

*#HopefulMinds #Hope #SHINEHope #FiveKeysToSHINEHope #GrowHope*
*#StrengthenHopeNetwork #PuttingMyselfInTheirShoes*

**LESSON 14 WORKSHEET**

# FINDING HOPE THROUGH FAILURE

Please tag us on social media @ifredorg to share your completed work and use the hashtags: #HopefulMinds #Hope #SHINEHope #FiveKeysToSHINEHope #GrowHope #FindingHope

# CONTROL THE CONTROLLABLES

**Directions:** List or draw the things you CAN control in the space inside the sunflower. List or draw the things you CAN'T control in the space around the sunflower.

#HopefulMinds #Hope #SHINEHope #FiveKeysToSHINEHope #GrowHope #FindingHope #HopeSupervillain

LESSON 15 WORKSHEETS

# SHIFTING RUMINATION THROUGH HOPE

Please tag us on social media @ifredorg to share your completed work and use the hashtags: #HopefulMinds #Hope #SHINEHope #FiveKeysToSHINEHope #GrowHope #RuminationToHope

# CHANGING THE CHANNEL

**Directions:** On the Rumination Screen, draw something that makes you ruminate. On the Hope Screen, draw something that allows you to change the channel and return to a hopeful mindset.

## Rumination Screen:

## HOPE Screen:

*#HopefulMinds #Hope #SHINEHope #FiveKeysToSHINEHope #GrowHope #RuminationToHope #ChangingTheChannel*

# LETTER TO MYSELF

**I. Directions:** In the space below, write a letter to someone in your Hope Network about something that you are worried about.

**Dear** _____ ,

_____
_____
_____
_____
_____
_____
_____
_____

**II. Directions:** In the space below, write a letter back to yourself about the Stress Skills and Happiness Habits you can use to help your worry.

**Dear** _____ ,

_____
_____
_____
_____
_____
_____
_____
_____

#HopefulMinds #Hope #SHINEHope #FiveKeysToSHINEHope #GrowHope #RuminationToHope #LetterToMyself

# MY HOPE JOURNAL

One great way to continue practicing your hope skills is through journaling. Think of your Hope Journal as a space to think about ways that you have activated your hope skills. Below are some journal prompts you can use to help start your Hope Journal.

1. How are you using your hope tools to succeed? Think about the SHINE acronym and how you've used it.

2. How has hope helped you overcome obstacles?

3. What SMART goals do you have for the future?

4. What can you control about the school year? What can't you control? How can you make the most of what they can control? How can you release emotions from what they can't control? How can you be creative about their experience this semester or year?

5. How do you define a hero? What do you think are some of the qualities in a hero? How does this person use hope tools in their life?

Please tag us on social media @ifredorg to share your completed work and use the hashtags: #HopefulMinds #Hope #SHINEHope #FiveKeysToSHINEHope #GrowHope #MyHopeJournal

# MY HOPE JOURNAL

# MY HOPE JOURNAL

Milton Keynes UK
Ingram Content Group UK Ltd.
UKHW051950180823
427131UK00009B/65